Polish Girls

Hot Sexy Polish Lingerie Girls Models Pictures

By **PHOTO ART LOVER**

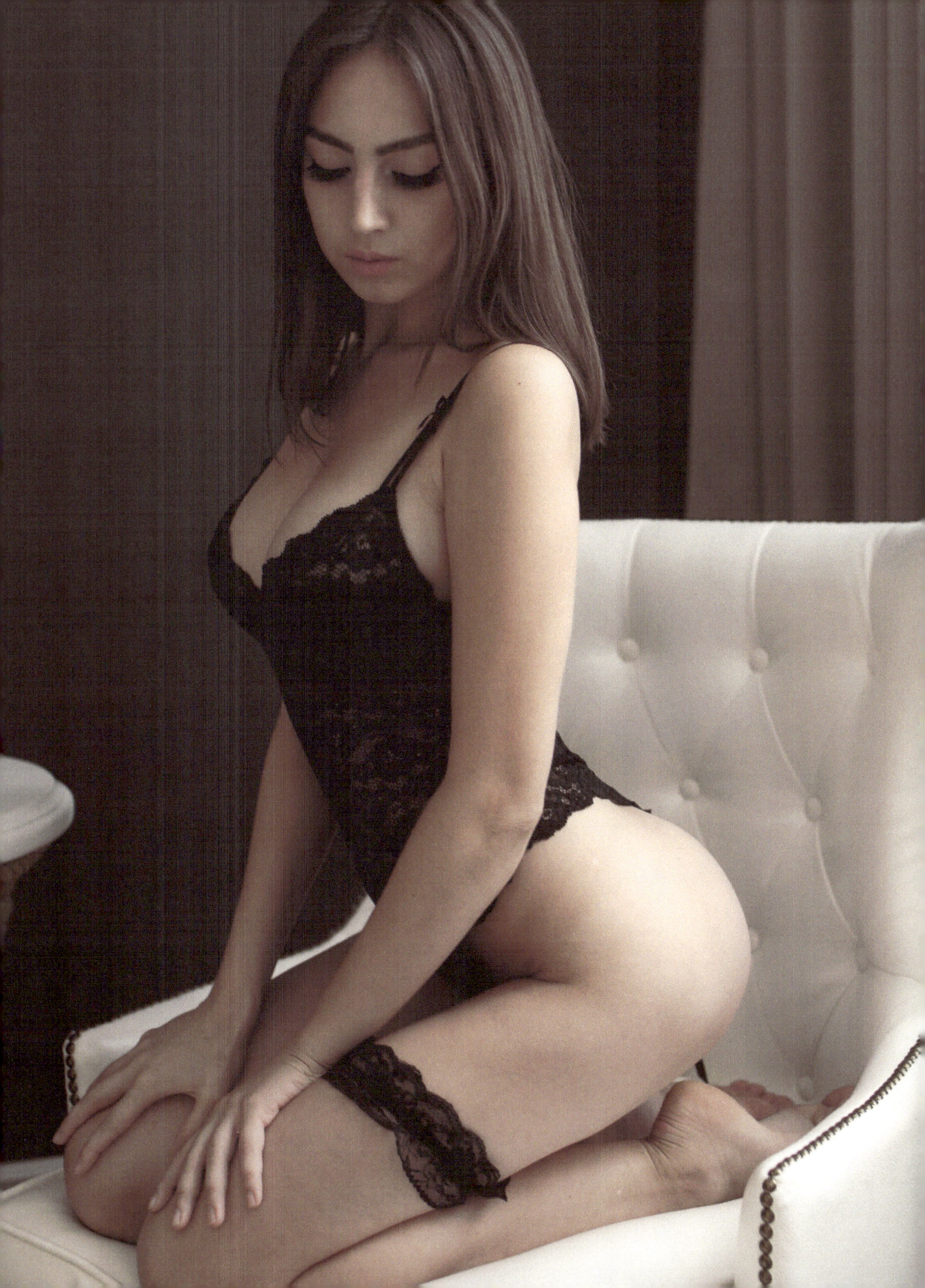

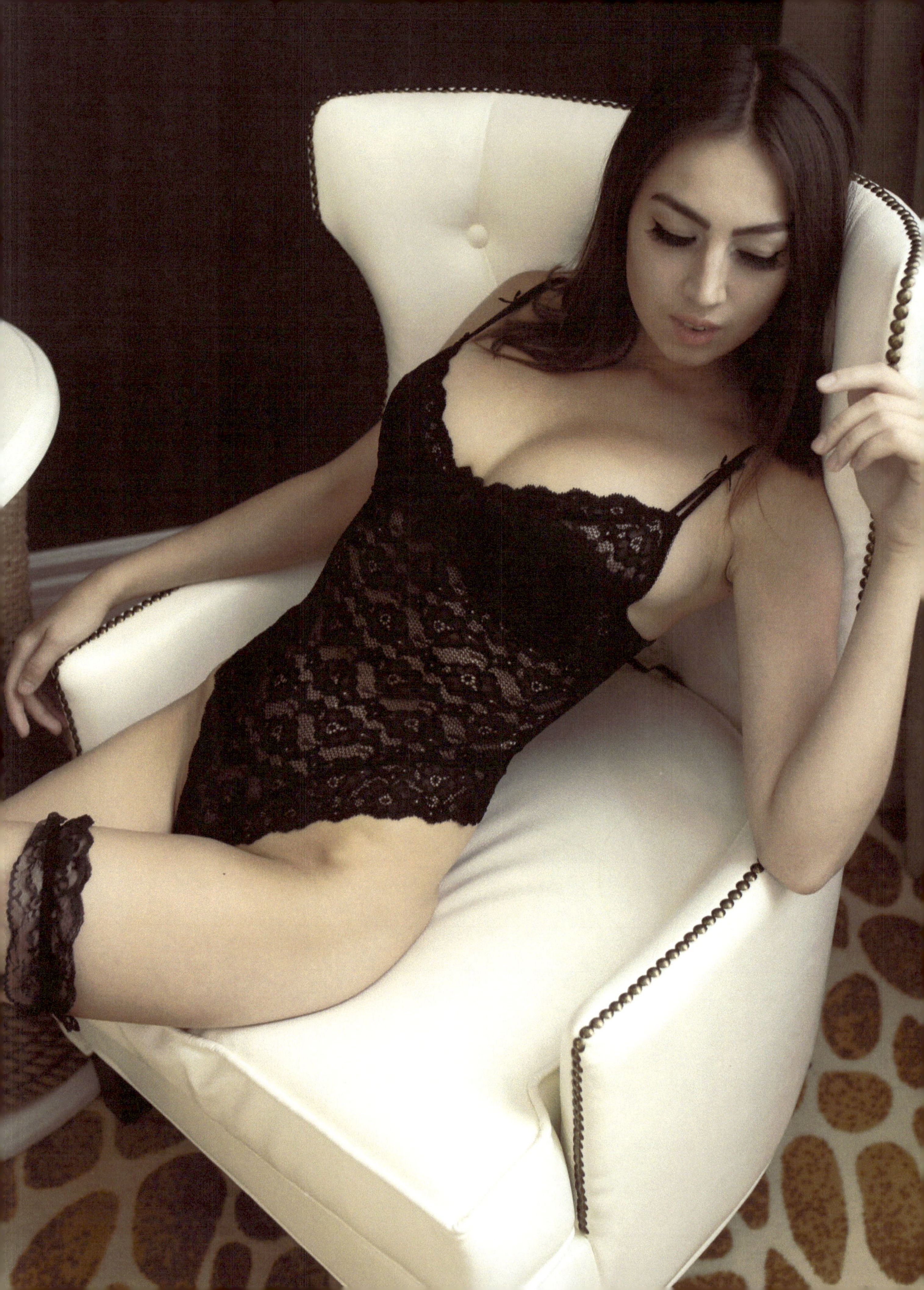

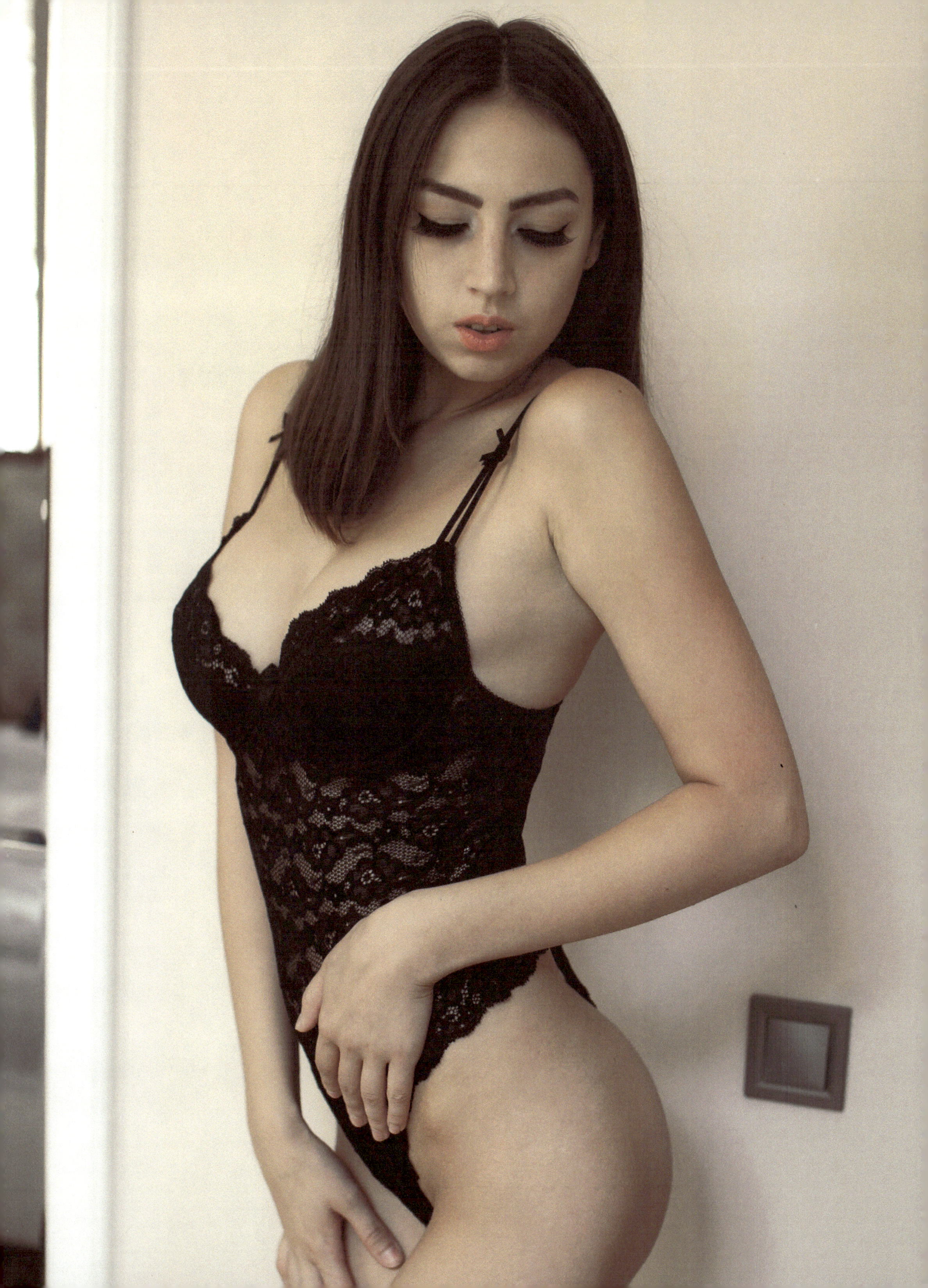

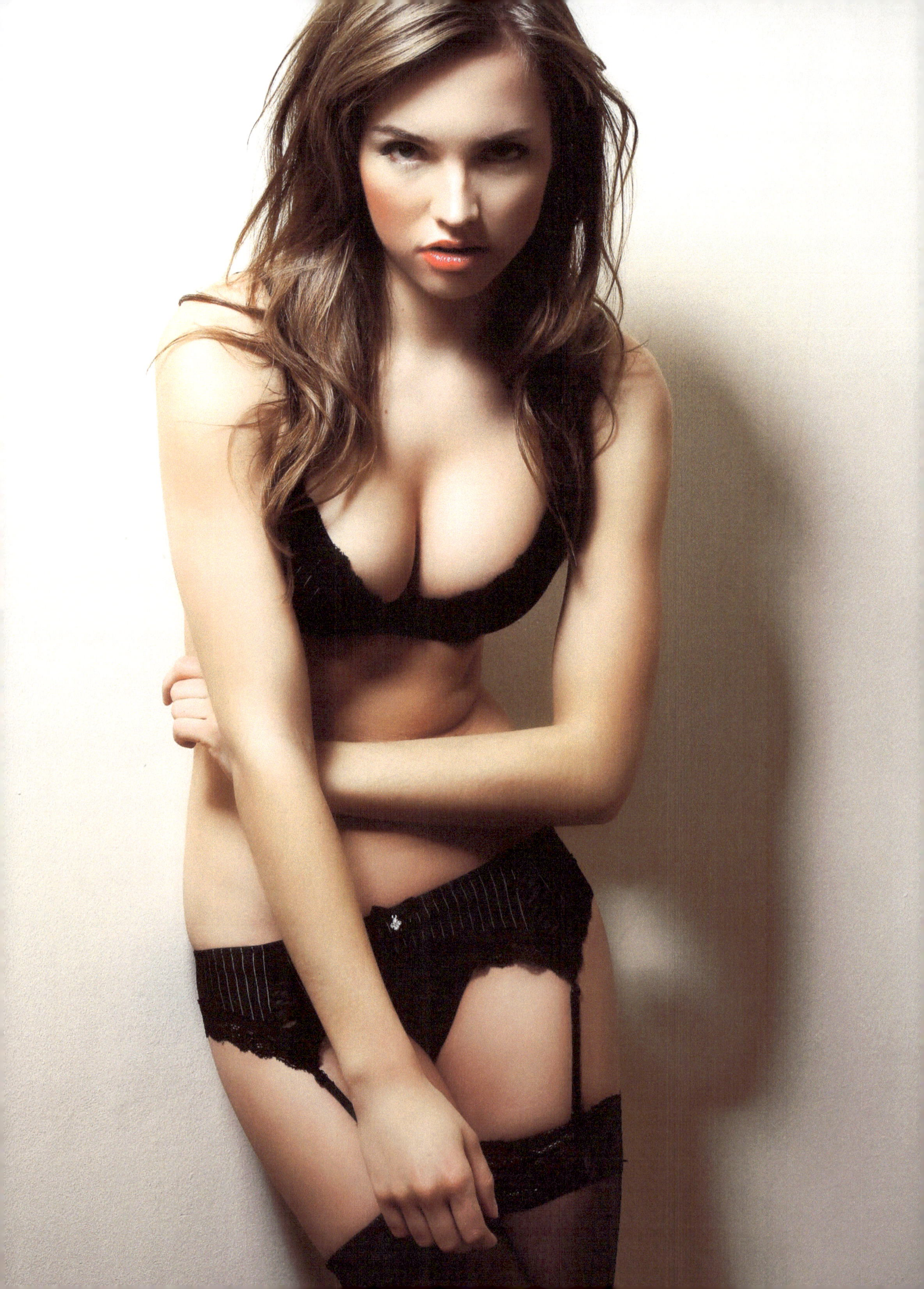

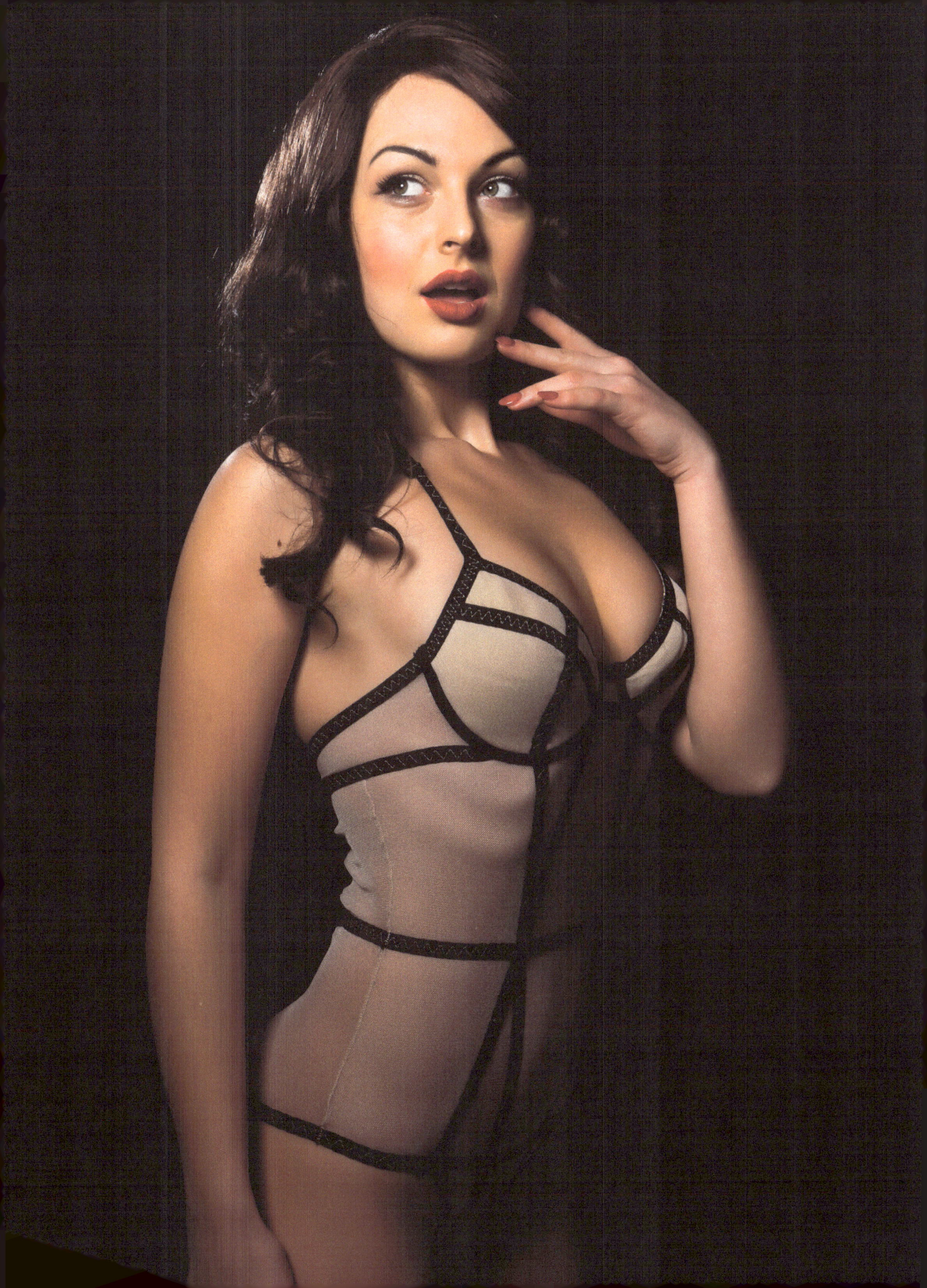

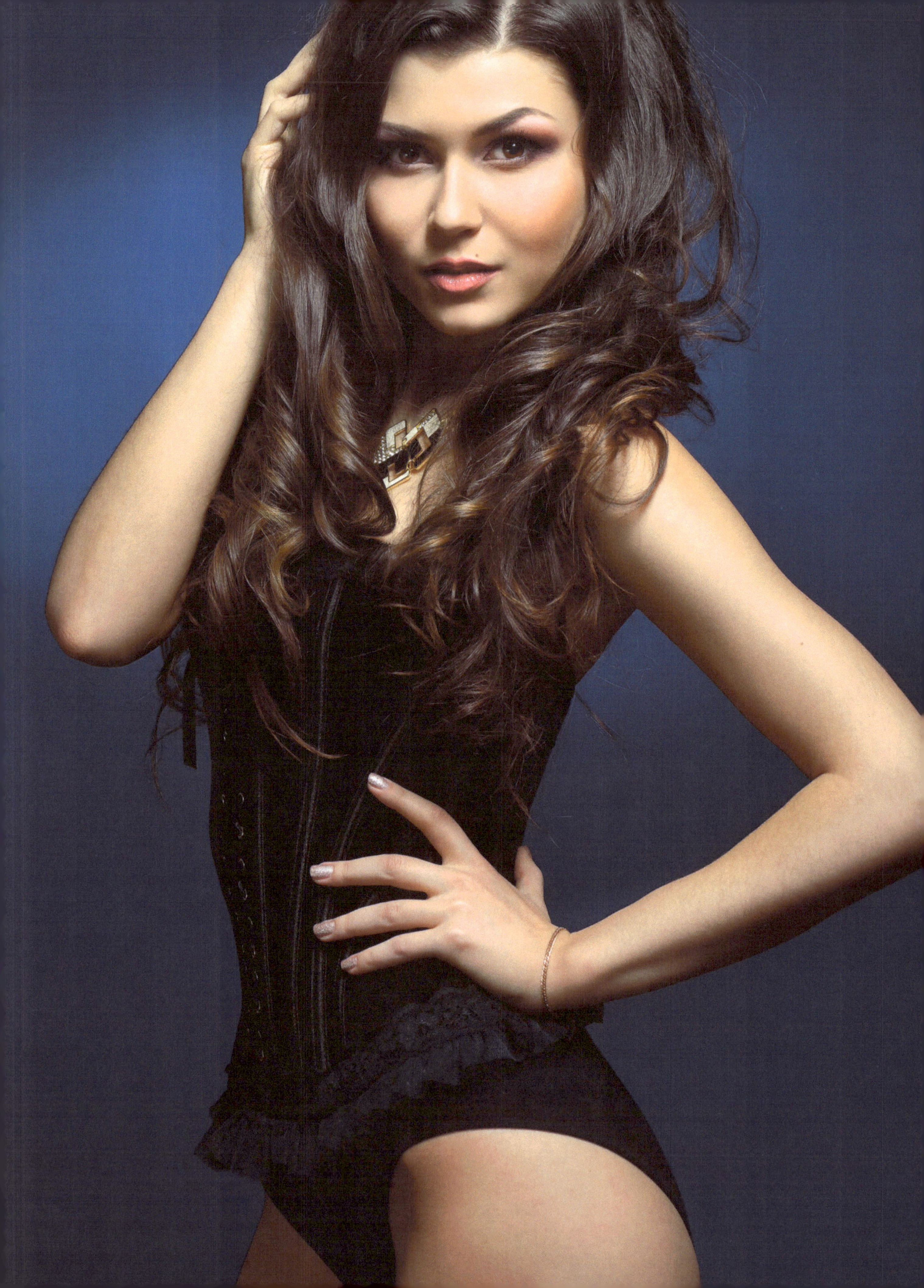

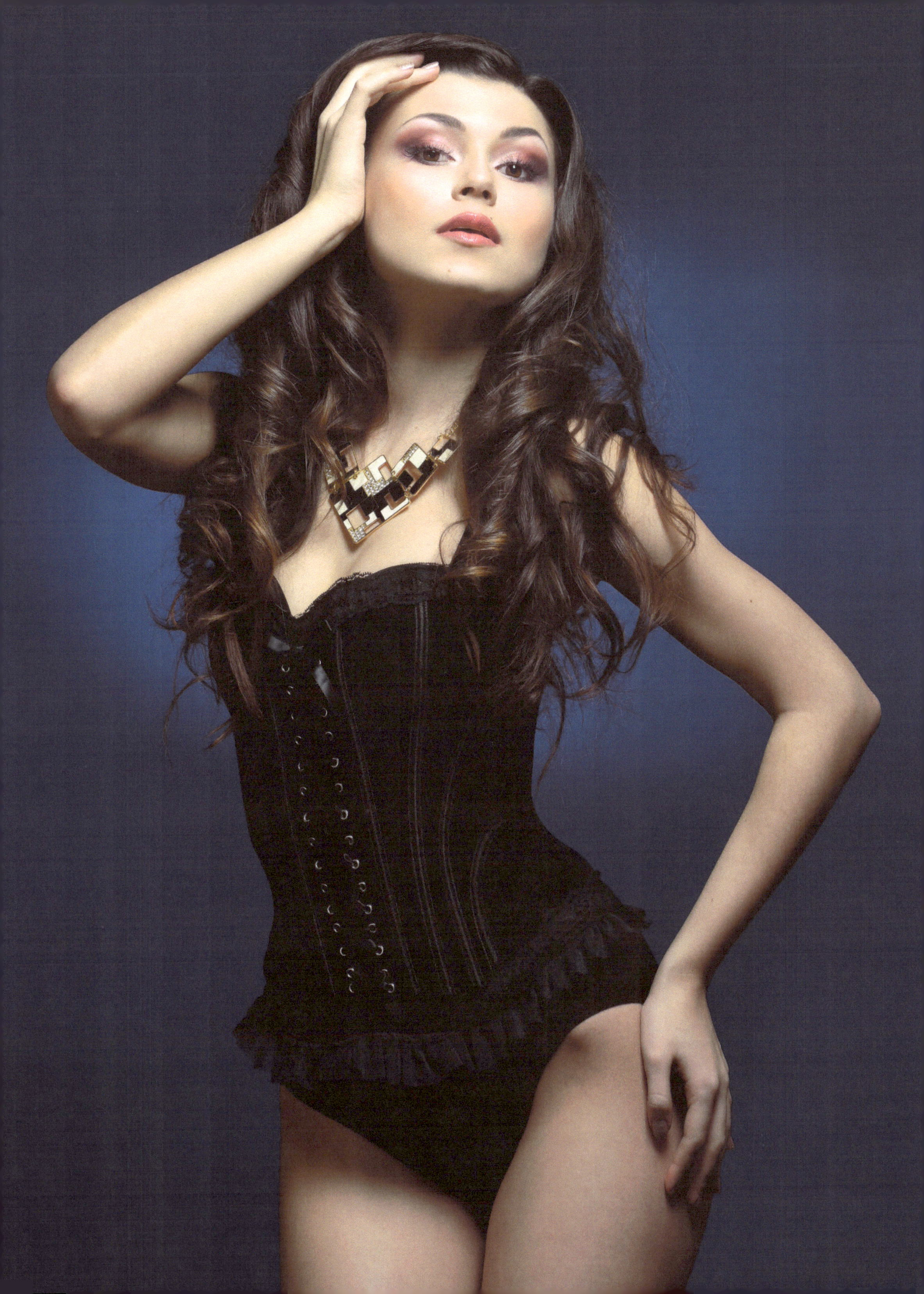

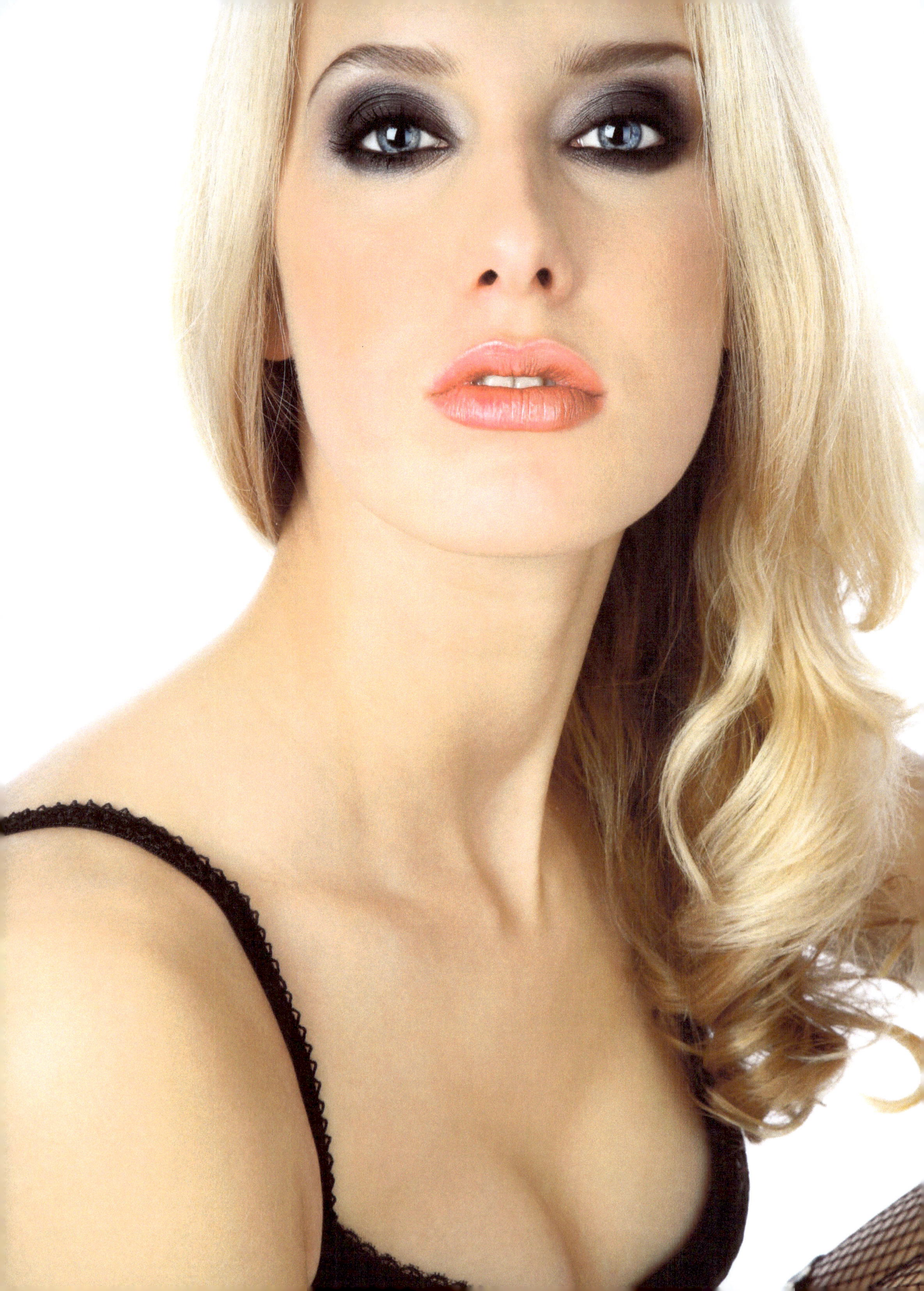

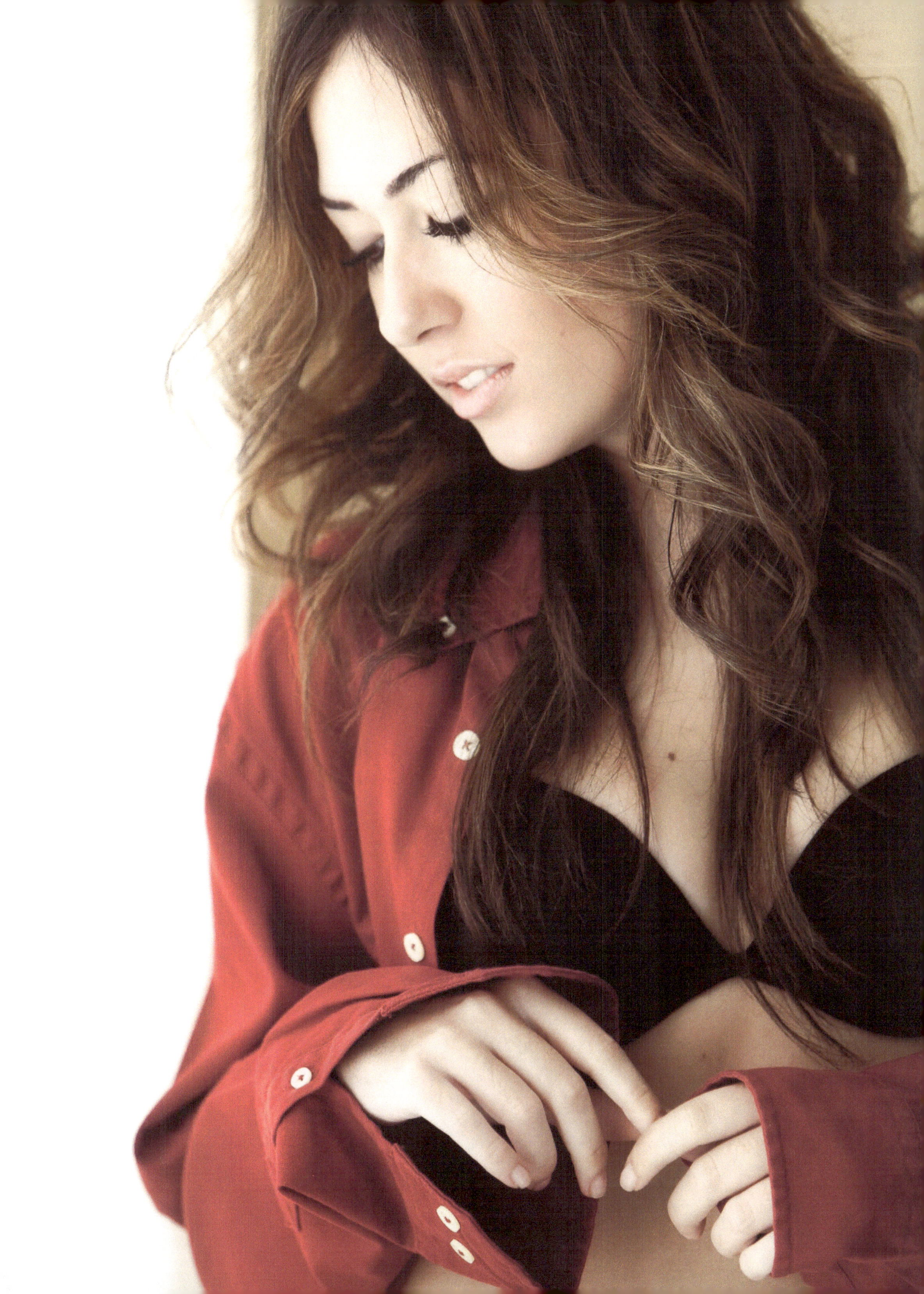

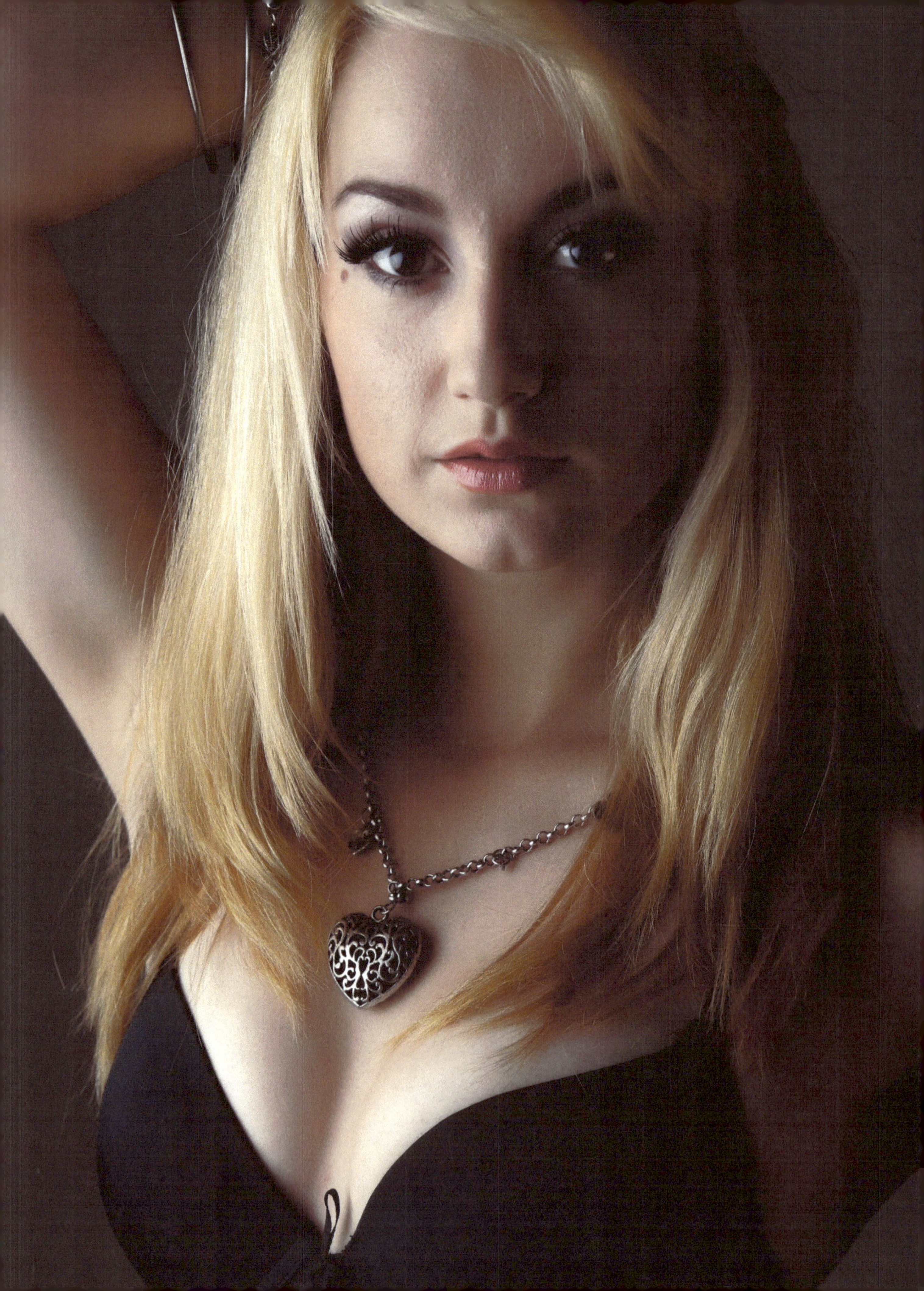

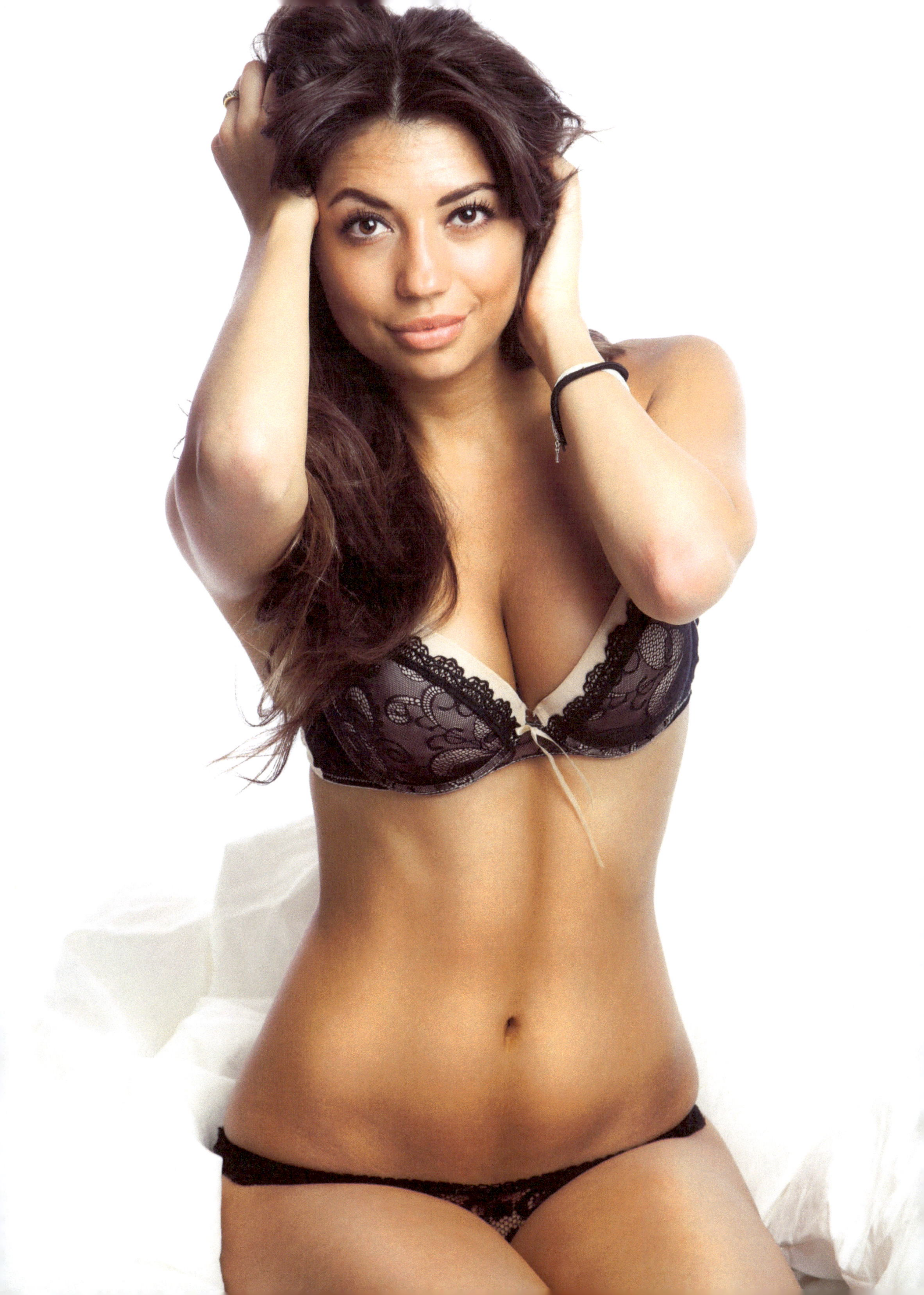

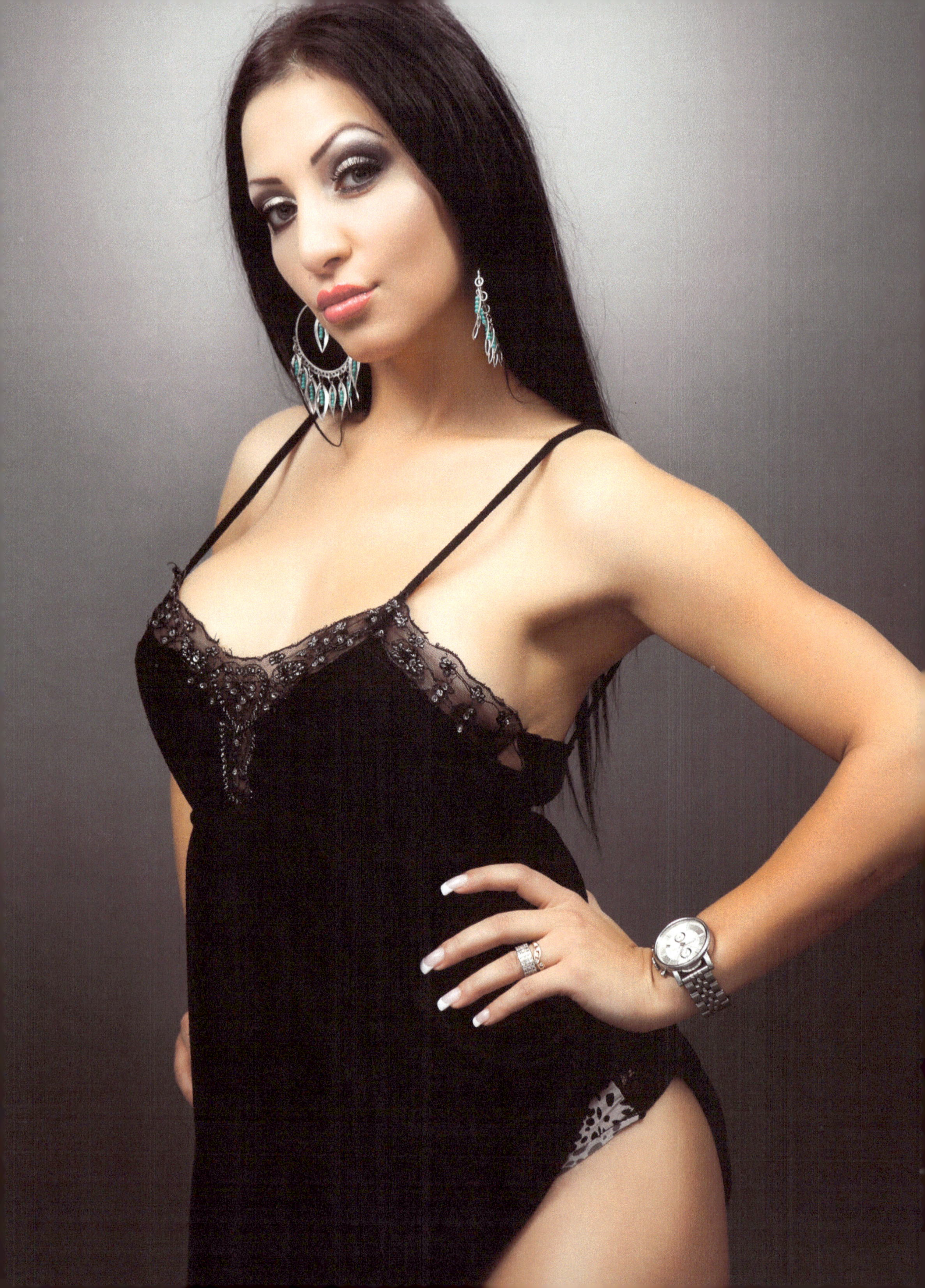

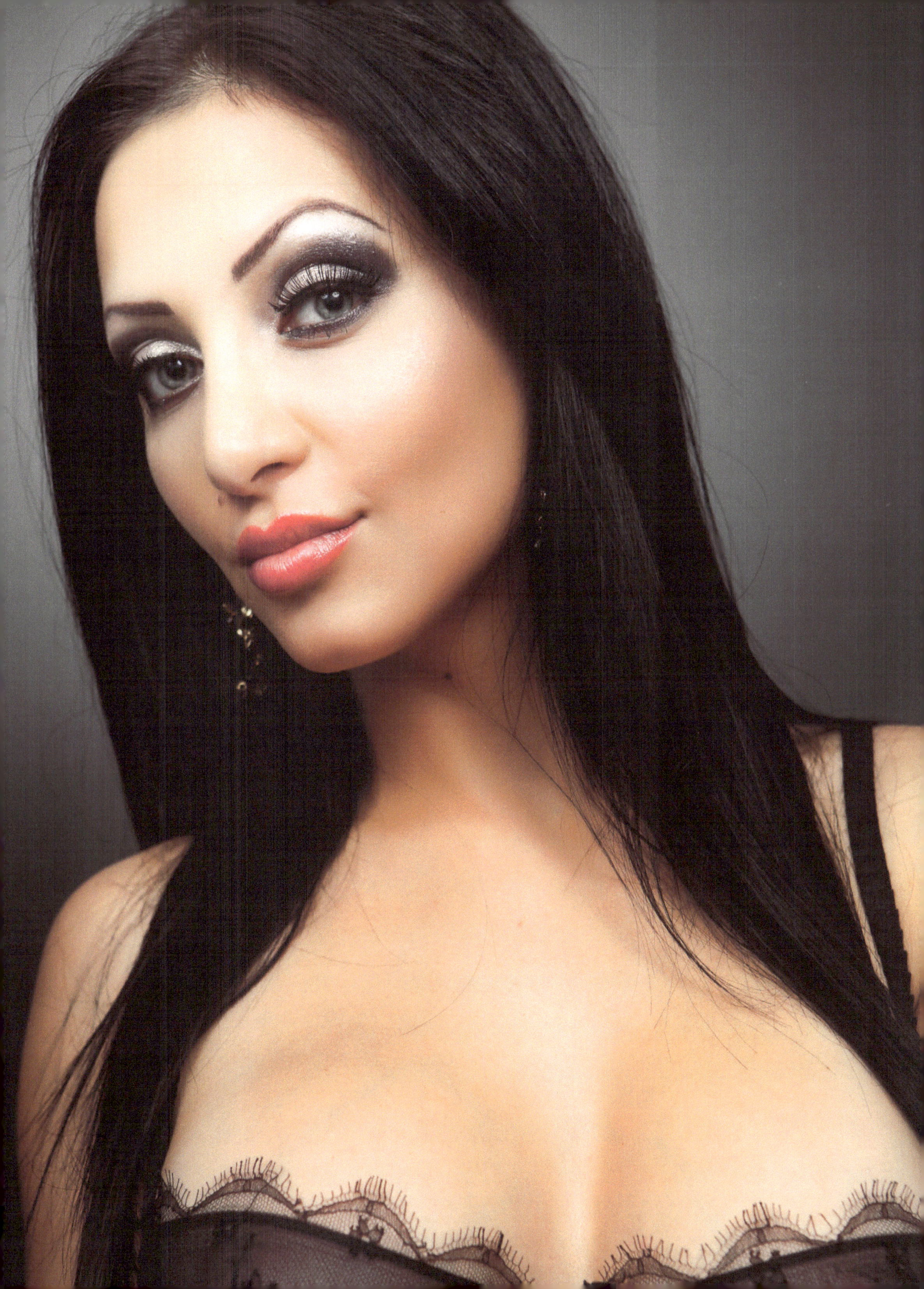

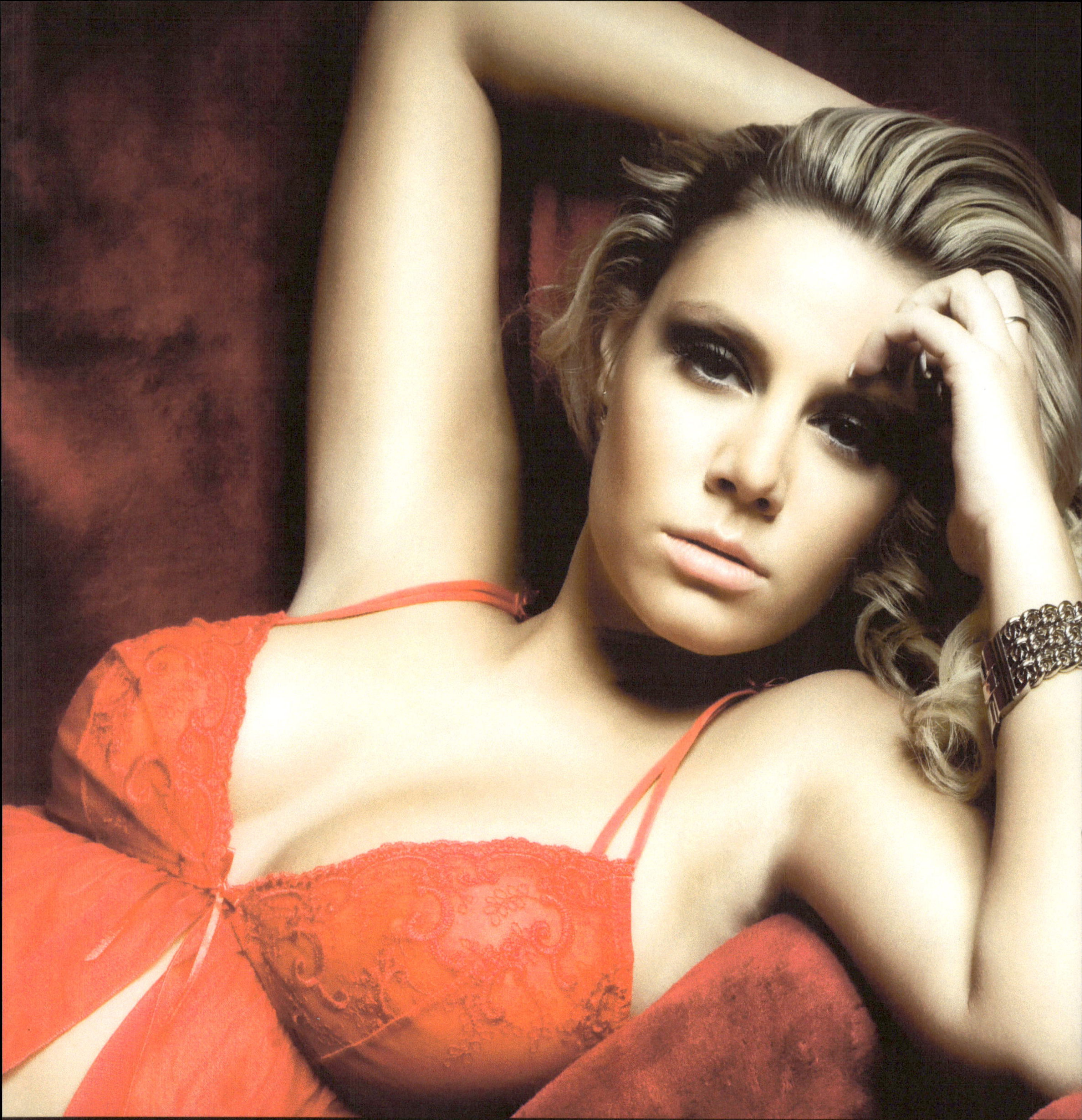

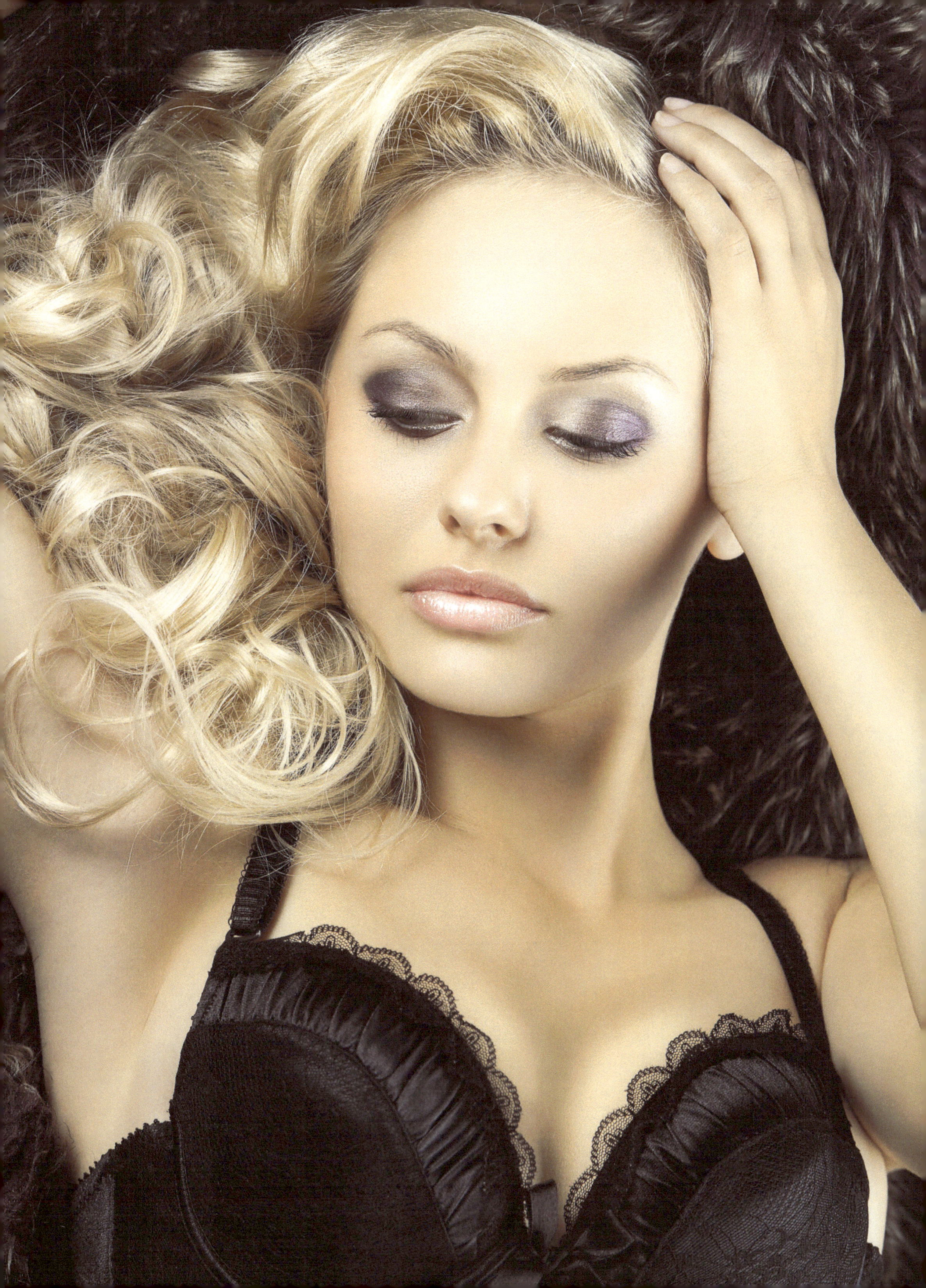

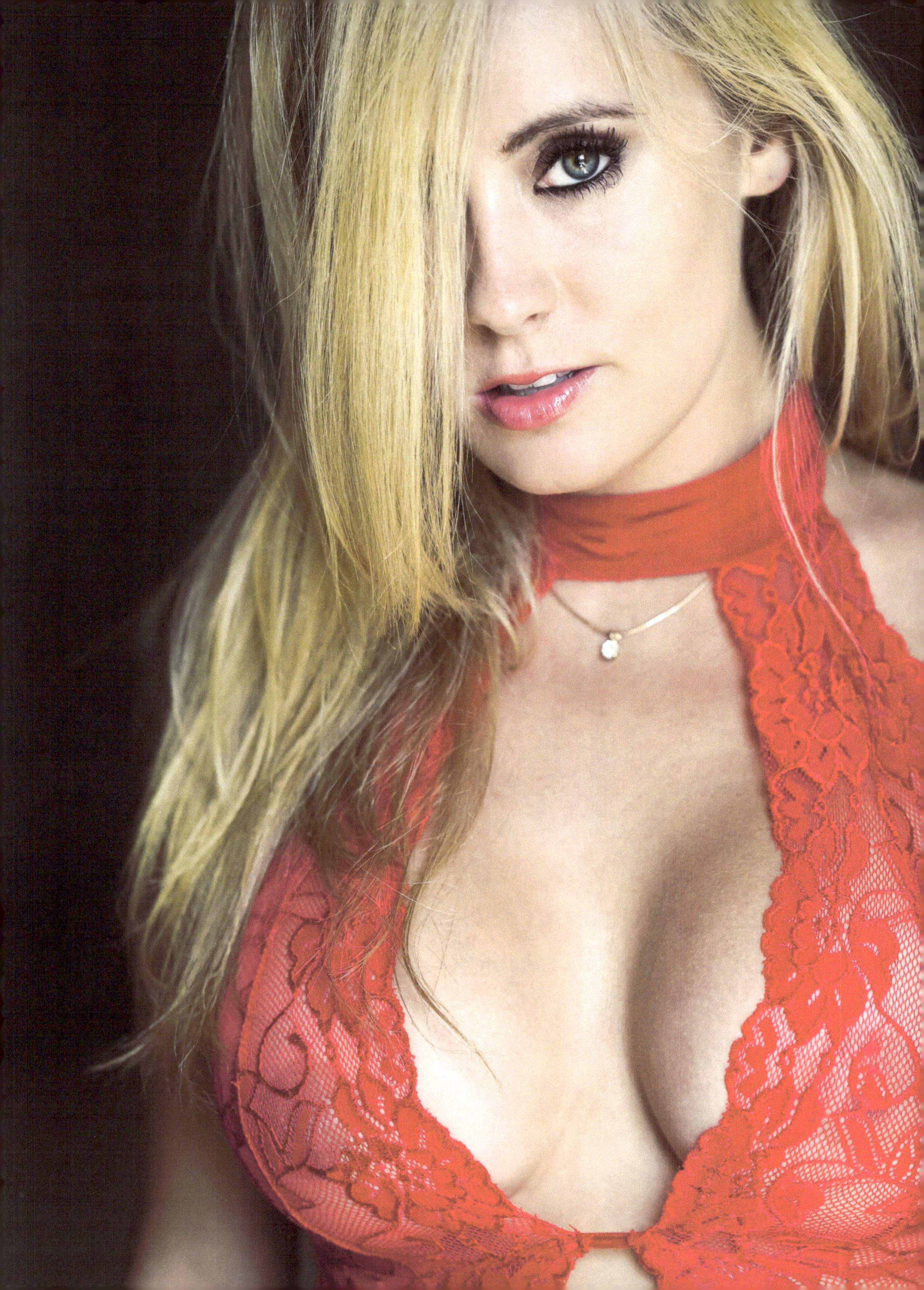

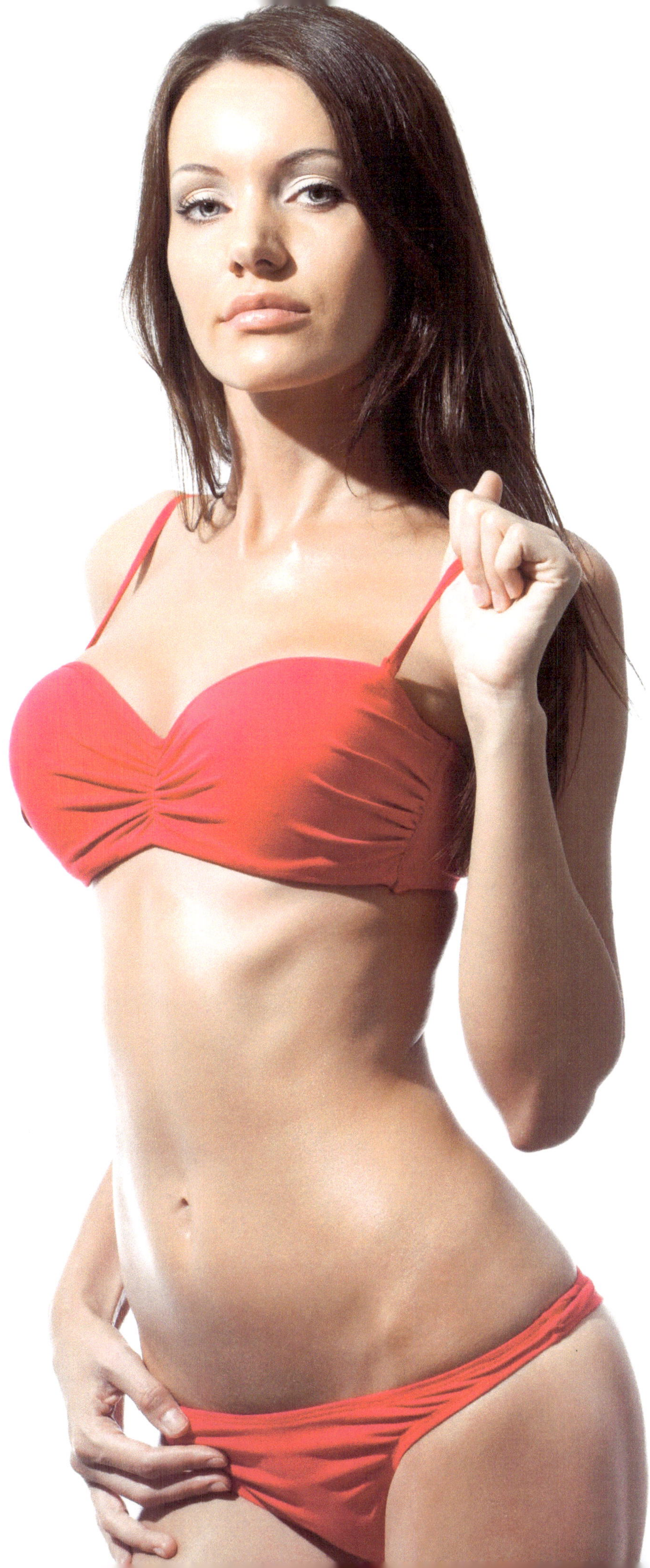

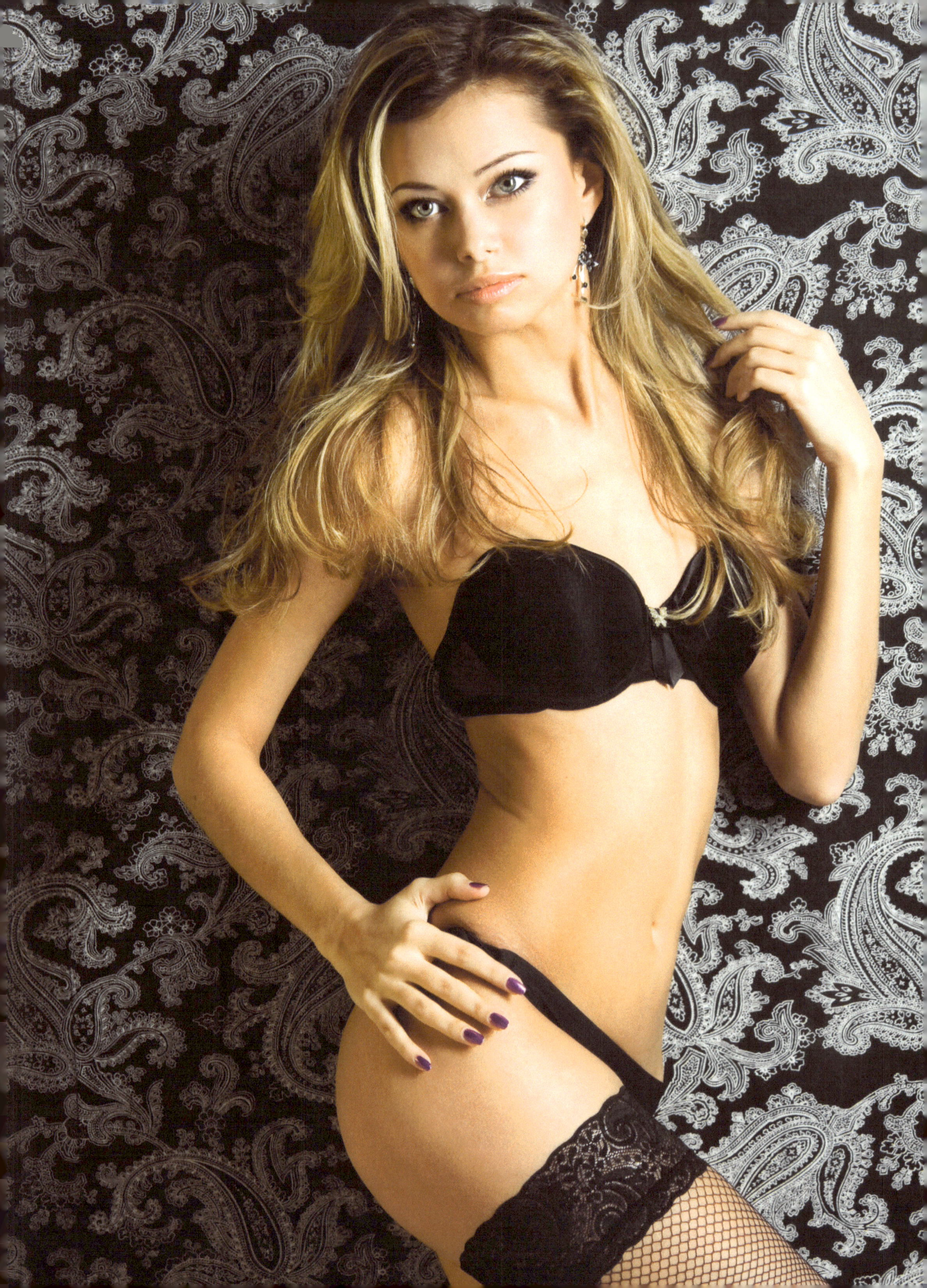

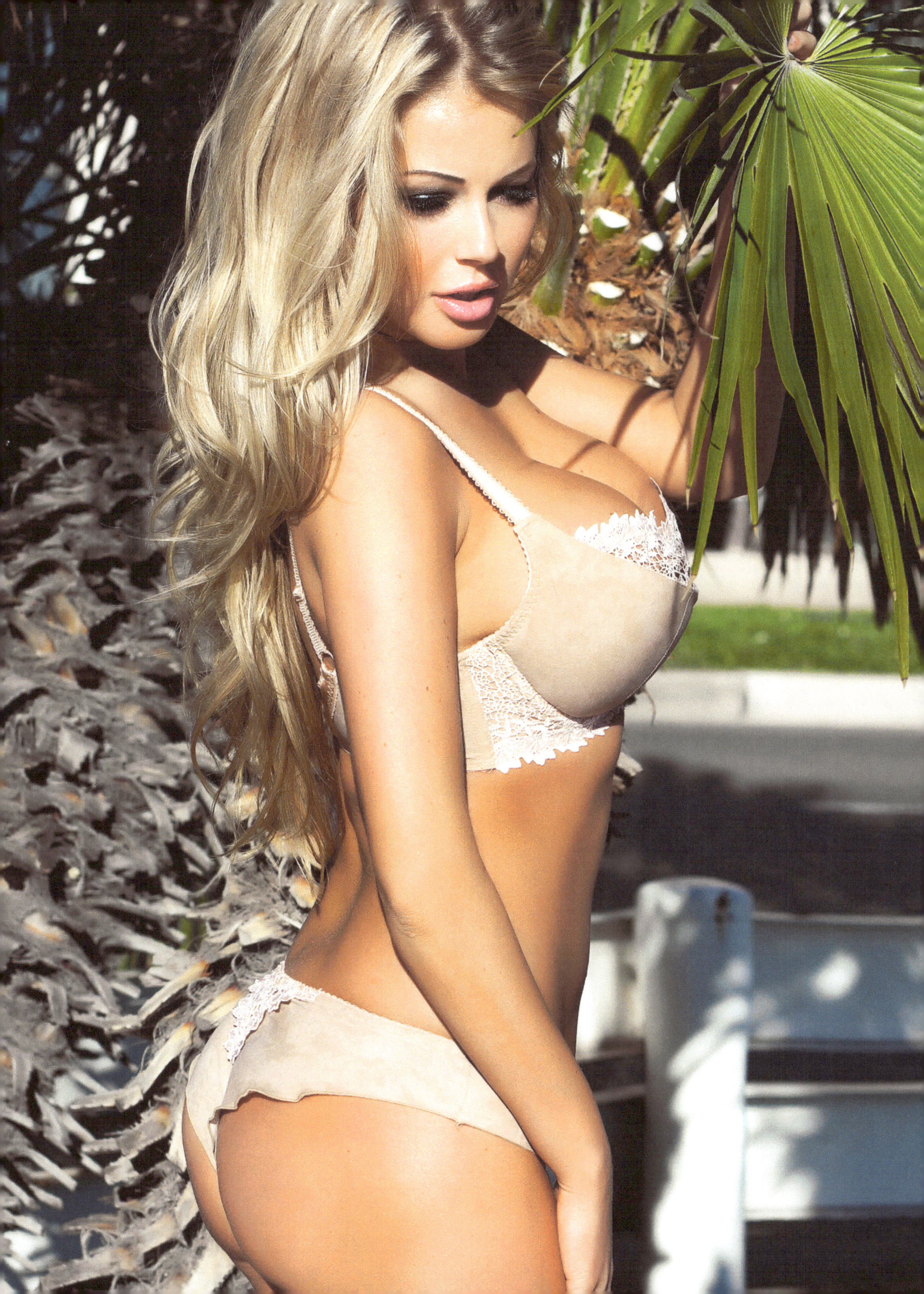

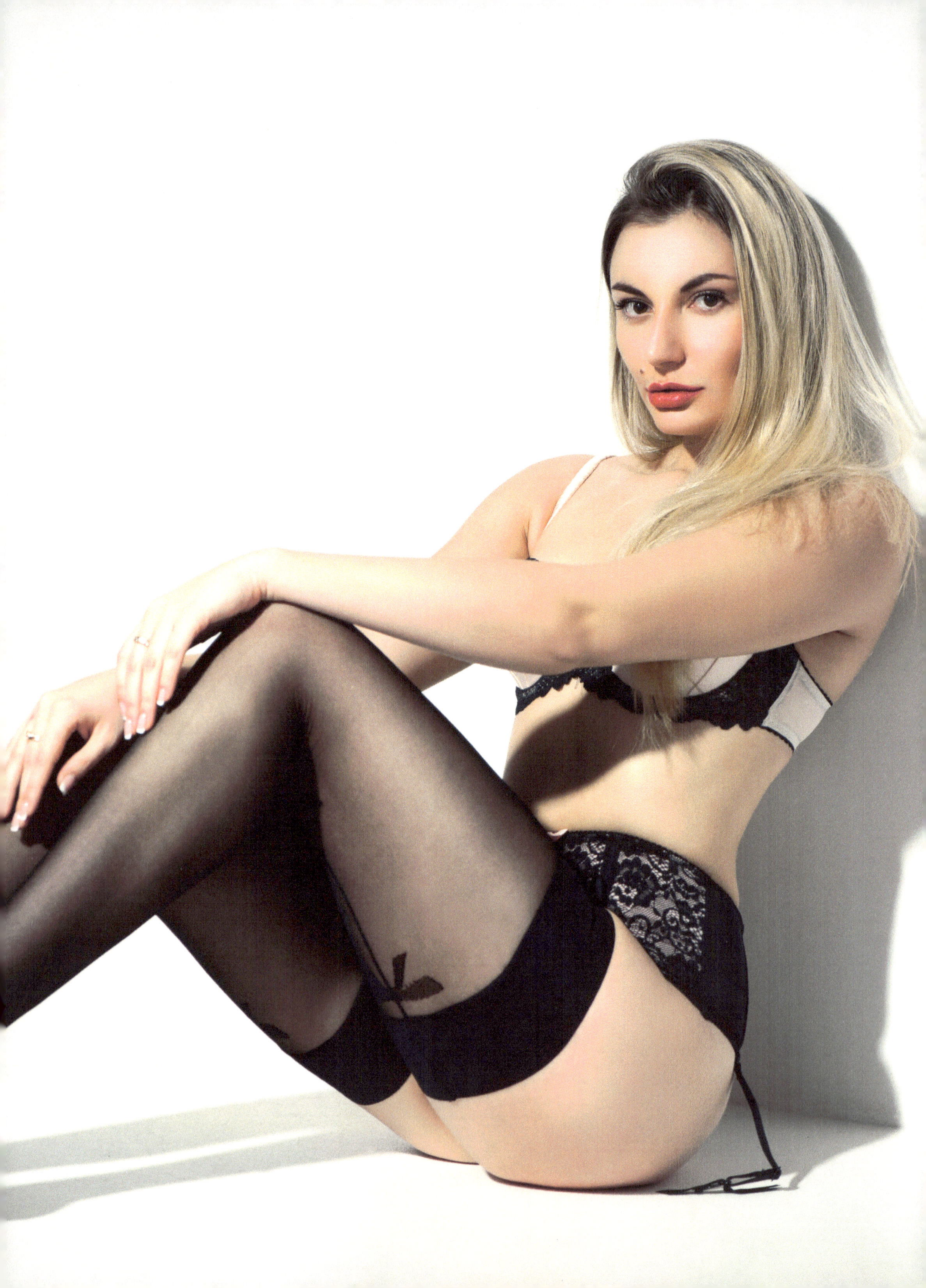

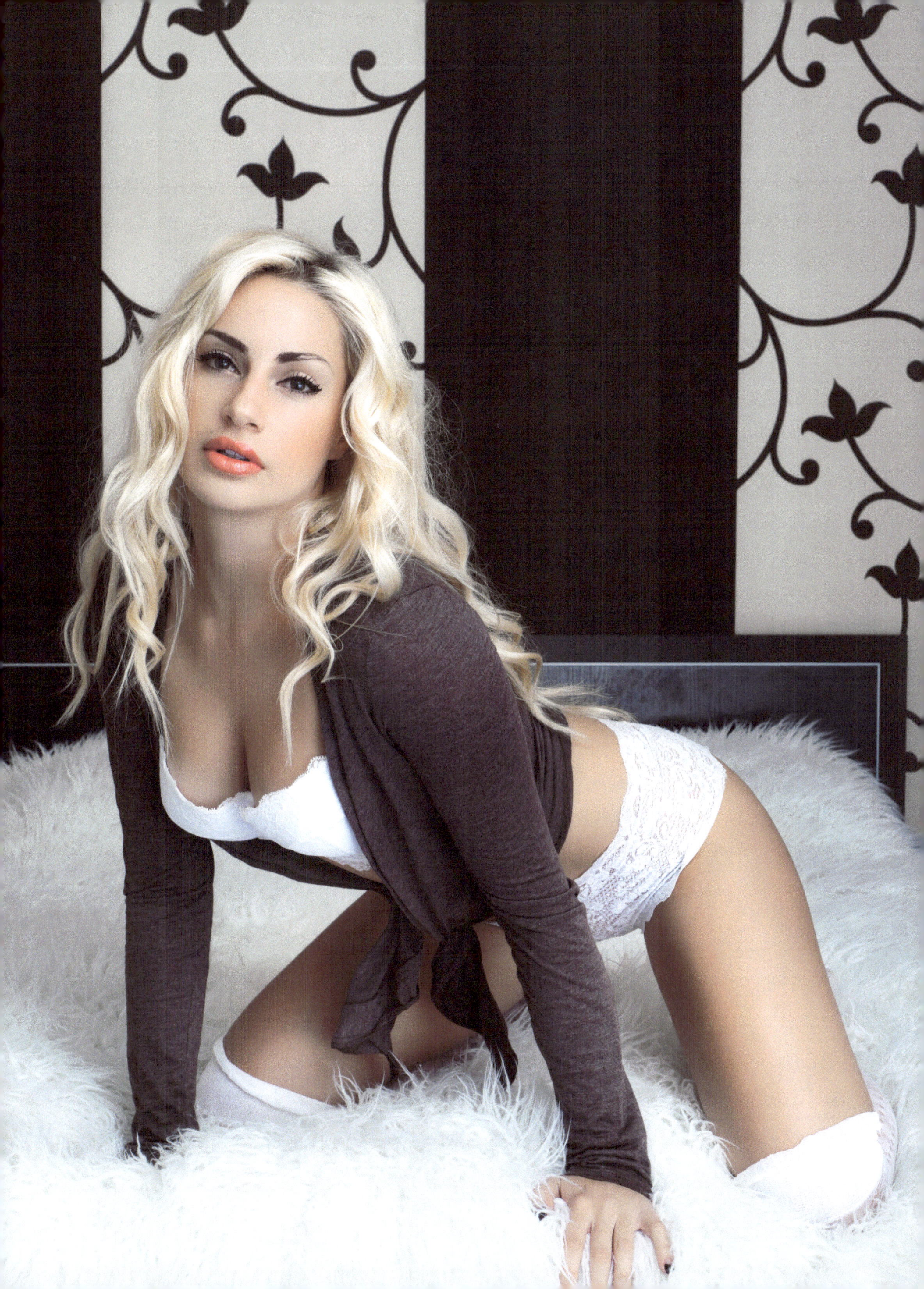

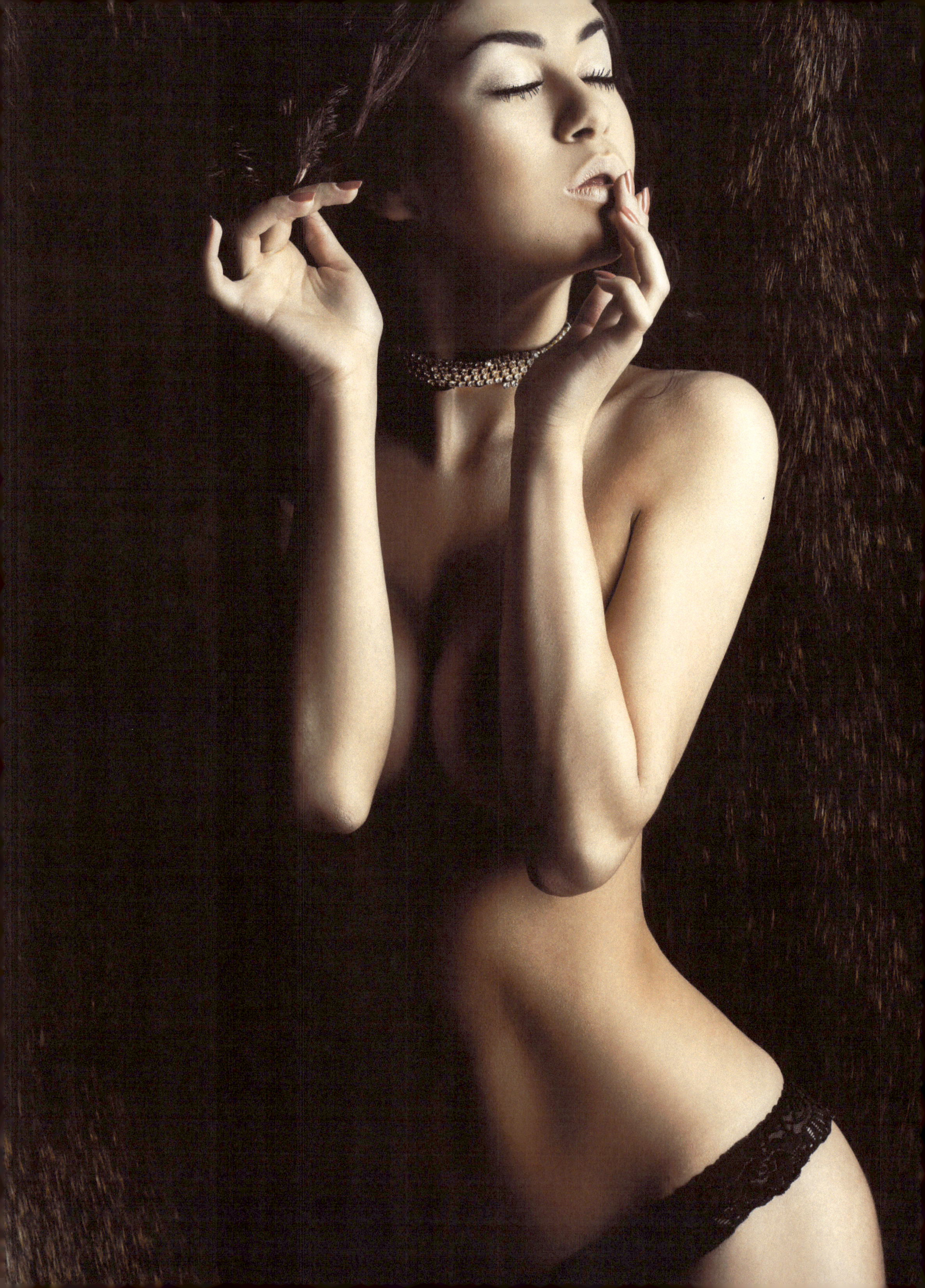

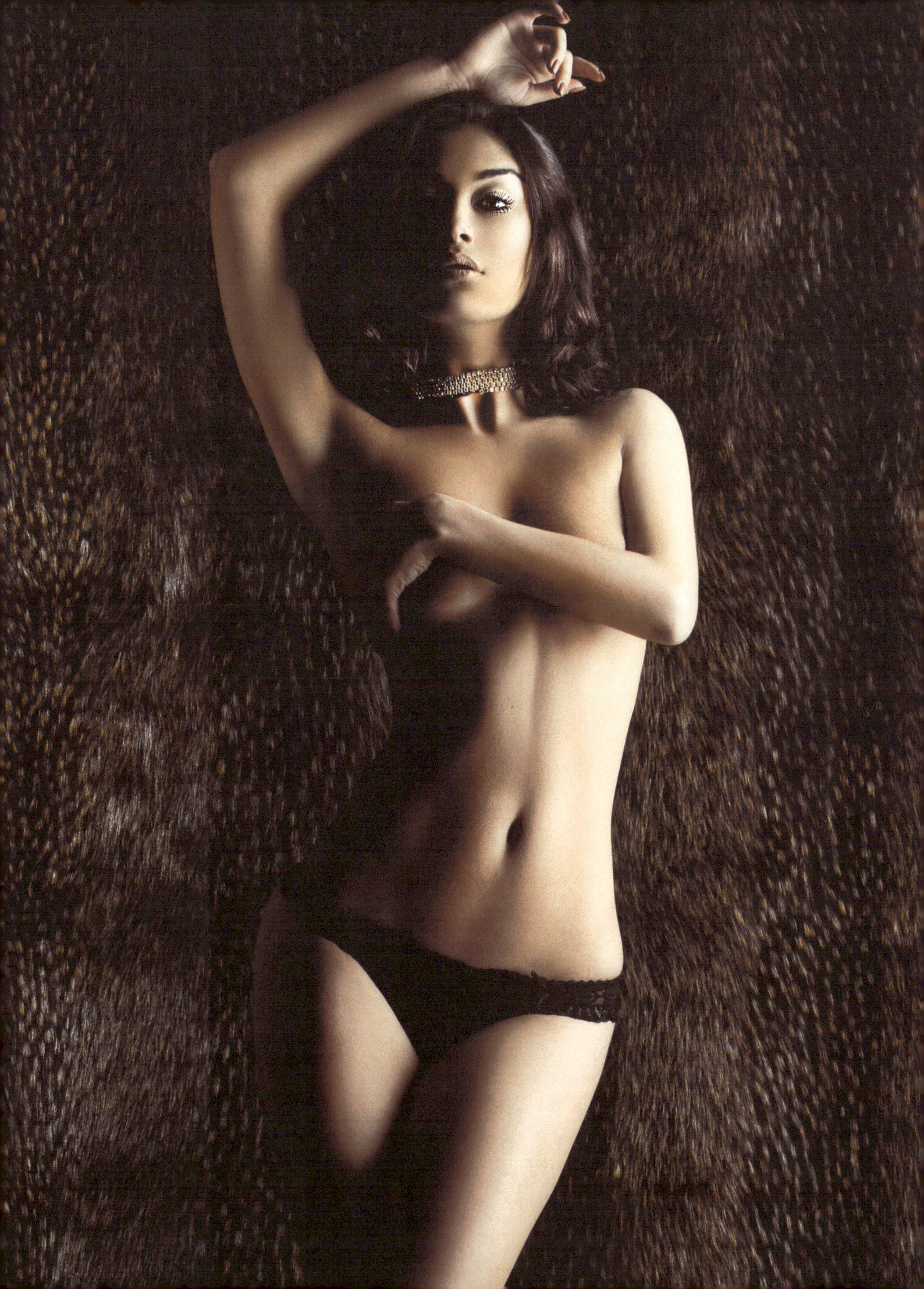

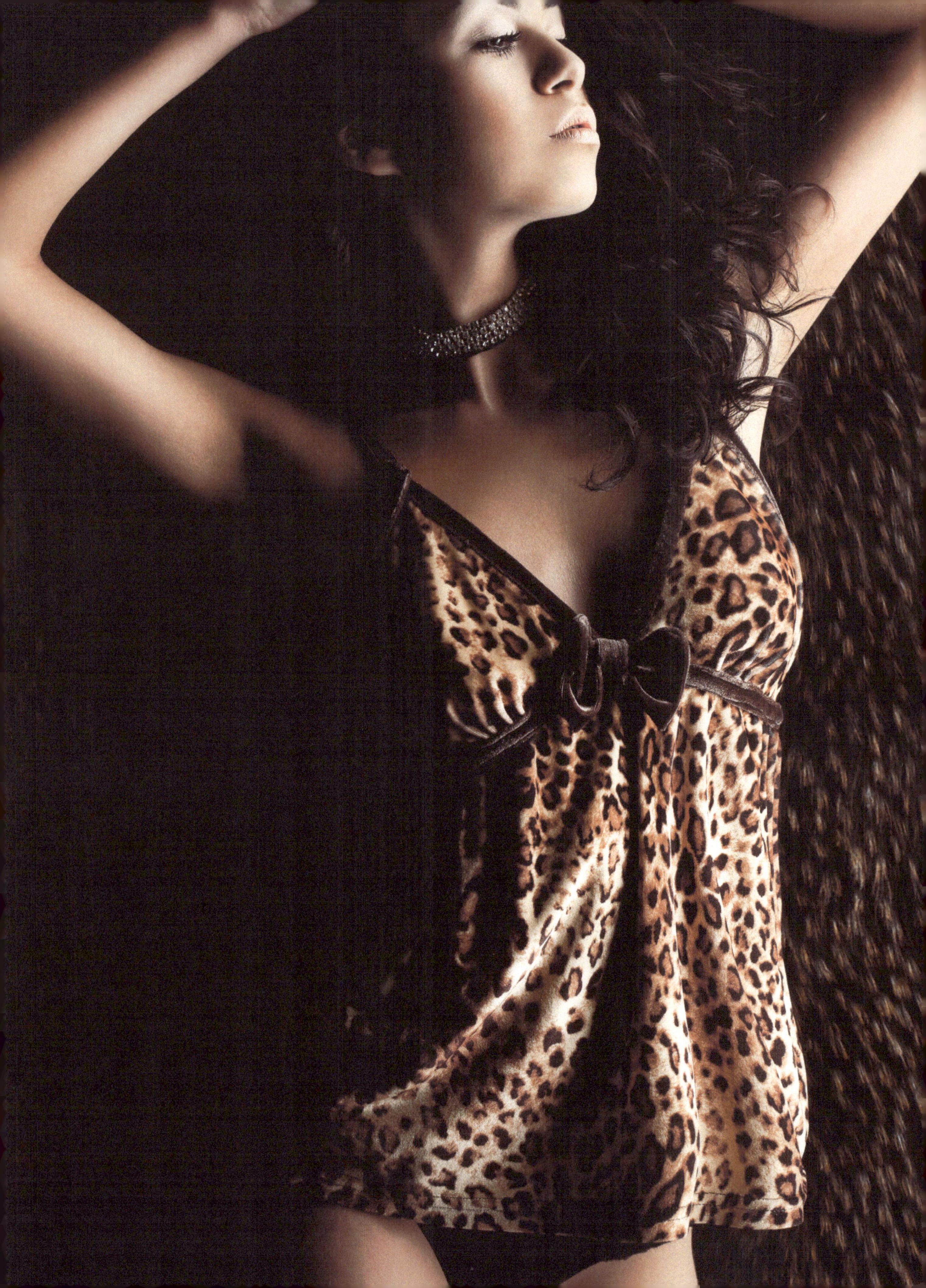

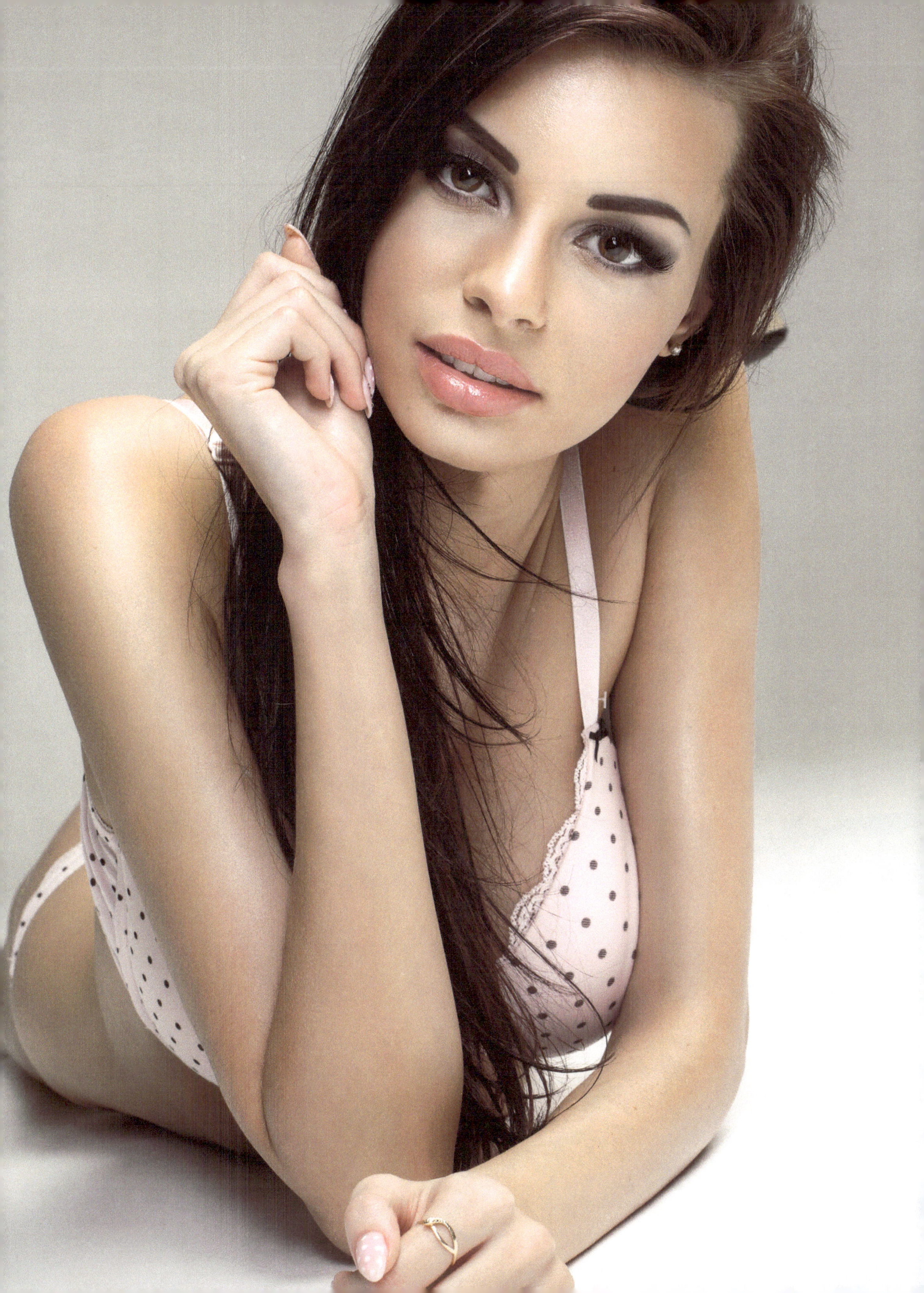

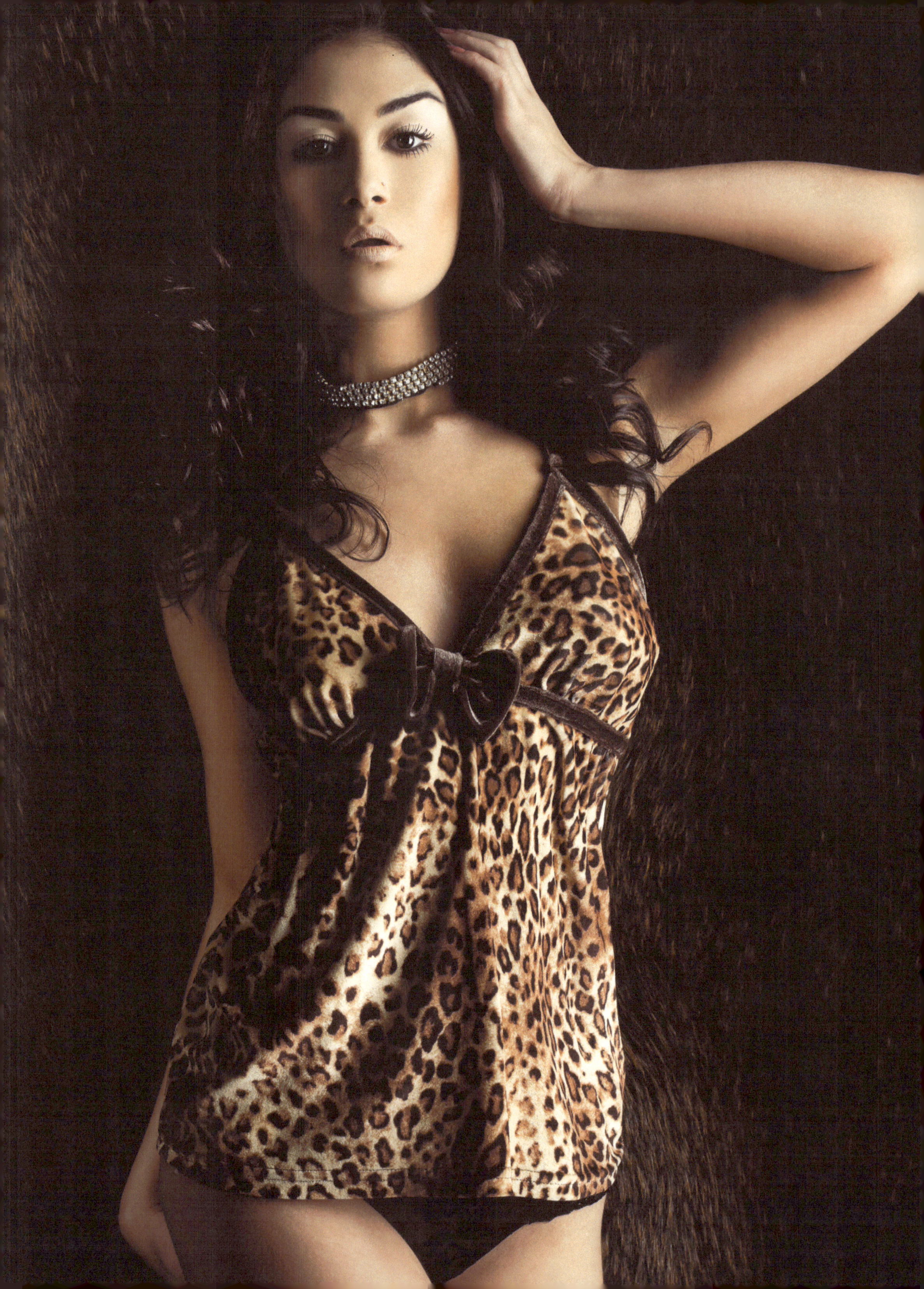

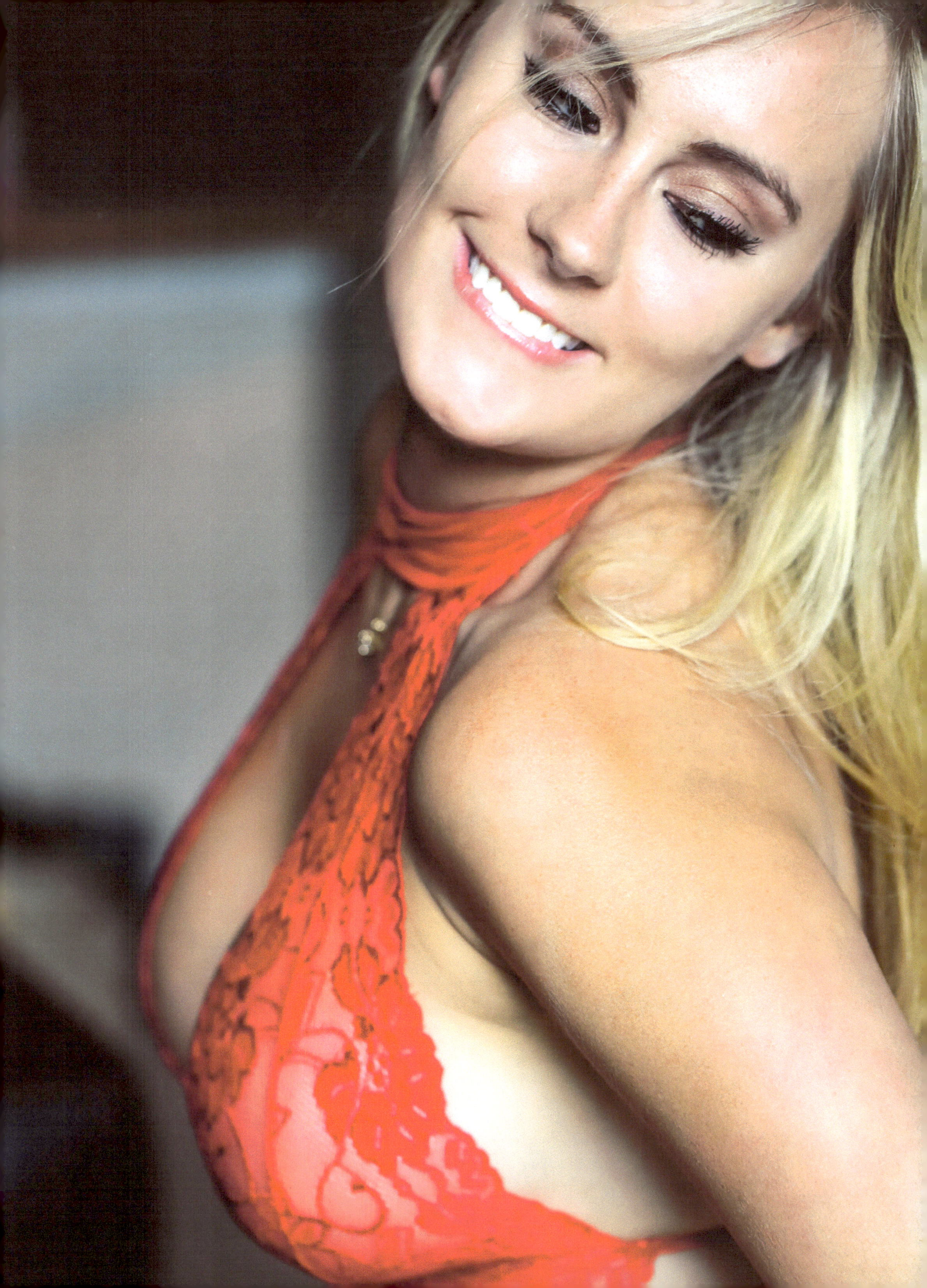

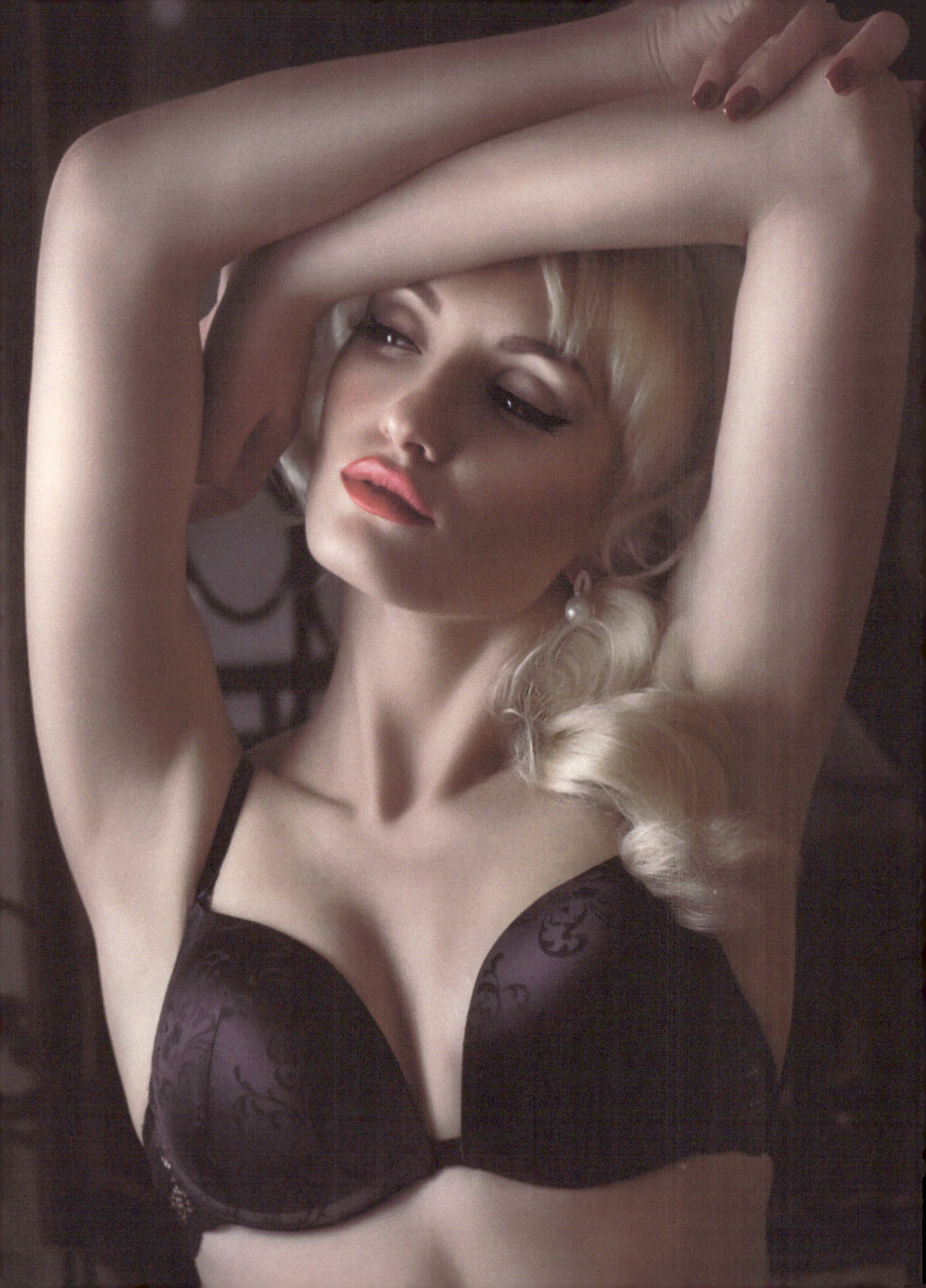

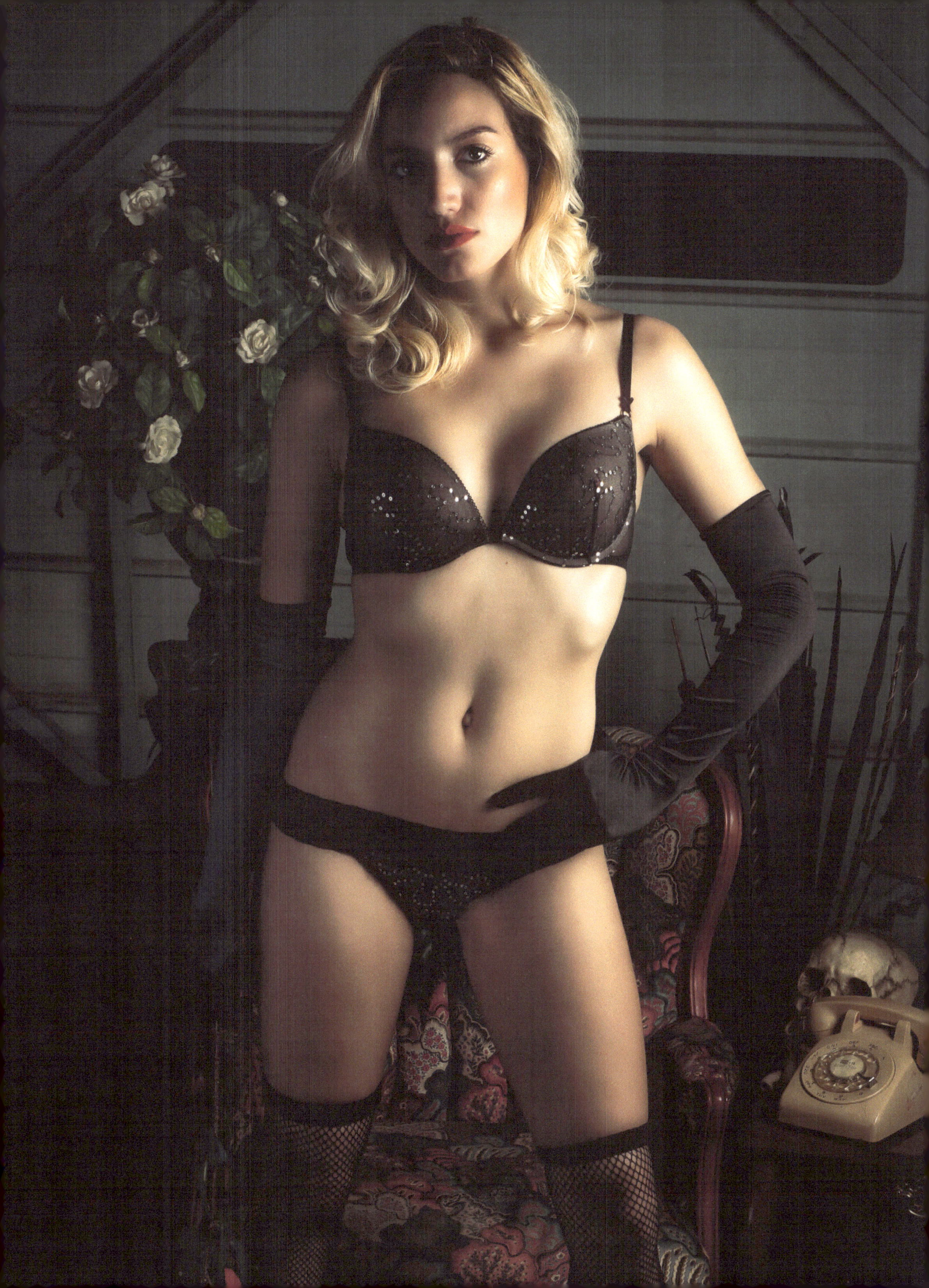

www.ingramcontent.com/pod-product-compliance
Lightning Source LLC
Chambersburg PA
CBHW050421180526
45159CB00005B/2358
* 9 7 8 1 5 3 9 0 9 5 3 8 5 *